COLUMBA

Poems by
KENNETH STEVEN

SAINT ANDREW PRESS

First published in 2005 by
SAINT ANDREW PRESS
121 George Street
Edinburgh EH2 4YN

Copyright © Kenneth Steven, 2005

ISBN 0 7152 0822 5

British Library Cataloguing in Publication Data
A catalogue record for this book is available from the British Library

Typeset by Waverley Typesetters, Galashiels
Manufactured in Germany by Bercker GmbH

CONTENTS

Poems in this collection have appeared in:

*Acumen, Agenda, The Countryman, Fire, FRAS,
The Herald, Island Magazine* (Australia), *Leviathan,
Life & Work, The Month, New Welsh Review,
New Writing Scotland, Nomad, Orbis, Planet,
The Scots Magazine, Tees Valley Writer,
University of Windsor Magazine* (Canada) and
Weyfarers.

⊠ COLUMBA

A film lies across the water meadows
like a muslin shawl. Birds lament
among rushes, their low voices trailing
like beads of glass. The sun has not been born yet,
remains under woods and hills.
Columba goes down, his ankles buried by soft water,
by green fronds, slippery, making no more sound
than a deer. The swans drift over the water,
so white they hurt the eyes. He stops,
forgetting everything as he watches the stoop and
        silver
of their grace, the sudden rippling of their backs
cast by wind, the furling of the huge wings
like shards of ice. They too are prayers,
personified, awakenings of God
in the morning water land.
He goes on, to the strange stone head
carved and lying dormant in the grass;
those wide eyes that never blinked,
the ringlets of stone hair curling
about the enigma of a half-buried face.
He comes here, even though the smiths who cut this
have known only gods of wood and loam,
have chanted under the wheels of stars,
made strange offerings of wheat and fire and gold.
Here at the water meadow's end he finds the Christ
ripe in his heart, his lips brim with words
that soar like larks into the sky,
almost as if some spring of light and joy

wells from the ground beneath.
He kneels in the wet softness of the earth
and smells the springtime yellow in his veins –
becomes the place he prays in.

❖ THE BURREN

It was the first of June
And late spring had blossomed into summer.
Along every lane sudden splutterings of larks
Rose in blinks against a blustery sun.

All the way from Lisdoonvarna to Kilfenora
Soft mauve orchids, crinklings of ferns,
The hawthorn bursting with white
Brimming with birds.

Life rising from limestone pavements –
Slabs of ice age left in the hills,
Like the chessmen on a giant's chessboard –
All the way to Ballyvaughan.

And I kept thinking I could hear the sea –
But it was the names of the villages,
Shifting and rising in my head,
Like shells in green water.

And I realised they had been there,
And this limestone and this life that filled it,
Since the day Columba left for Scotland –
A thousand springs ago.

❖ Whatsoever Things

I

The Watcher
Out on the very west
On a ridge of rock
In the darkness.

Below him
Sea dragons and spumes
There where the waves
Crash on the stones.

The Watcher knows the stories
Of the longships;
The men hammered out of the north,
Threading the storms

To trample on villages
As if they were grapes,
Rip stone from stone
Till they find the glint

Their eyes thirsted;
The clink of silver, of gold –
Fashionings –
To row back home once more.

The Watcher shivers
In the grey beginnings of dawn,
Islands being born from the bleakness,
Second by slow second.

He fingers the one coin
The monks paid to buy him –
To buy his watching
Through the long, dead night.

And he thinks of her
In the softness of her sleep
The curve of her breath
The gold at her temple –

He touches
The beautiful pain of longing,
Of waiting and watching,
Knowing homecoming

Will find her.
Yet he wonders, there, as he watches,
Which is more delicious –
To wait, or to find.

II

This is where the book is being made –
Up here, in the stone eyrie
Set out against the west
Like a boulder in a dyke.

How many hundred years
Have poured into its pages?
How many hands
Gave the beat of their hearts to its light?

All of it for the man of Galilee;
His story of wood and nails
That snagged them, tore them
With love and wonder.

The stone gods lie in the grass
Broken and dead,
Left behind,
Blinded now by the sun.

More than everything in the world
These monks are workers of words;
Men of letters
In love with nibs and inks.

And here, in the rattle of the west wind,
Crippled with winter cold,
They crouch in a flutter of candle,
And form their gospel.

III

Yet it is the girl I see
This February,
High on the moorland
Where the myrtle and the cotton grass

Blow in the first blue wind of spring.
It's her I see,
The young girl from the island
Gathering flowers,

Tiny edges of things
Crouching out of reach of the wind –
Emerald and red and mauve –
Little glens of flowers.

She sings to herself
Soft vowels of song –
Something Columba sang
In the great echoes of the stones.

This is her service
This is her Sabbath –
The gathering of the flowers
In the early blue of the year.

She does not notice
The day's passing –
That is what love means
To give and not count the cost.

In the low light of evening
When Calva and Inch Kenneth redden
In the last breath of sunlight
She rises and walks back

Her baskets full of flowers
Her eyes full of prayers.
She takes them to the place
Where the book is being painted;

She asks no reward
For what she gives,
Knowing she has been given
Tenfold in return.

Night falls. A curl of moon
Floats into the open sky
West of Ben Mor.
There is nothing else

But the lone man in his stone fastness
Finding the single flow of a letter
In the page of his parchment,
The moon blessing his hand.

❖ PENWITH

Nothing in the world could prepare you for a
    January like this –
Penzance huddled in a corner, its flags at half-mast.
The yachts in the harbour clinking and rocking
In the huge grey beast of the wind.

But inland, something else is here beside
The broken walls of the tin mines, the inked miles of
    strangeness
That wade into moorland on the edge of the sky
That has no trees, that has no heart.

The colourlessness of the land shudders –
The sun has been washed into the sea. The only light
Lies in the lions that roar and roar
Over the huge gold of Porthcurno's sands.

Except at Crean, for a moment, when something
    lifted and I looked –
A fistful of goldfinches burst like flowers
From the magic of the air and promised
Resurrection, a second chance.

ORKNEY

Everything important, they say, blew away
A long time ago. The eyes don't need much
To imagine longships unfurling their anger in these
    bays;
Each island breathes its history easily, effortlessly.
The children are unselfconscious, they go in huddles
Down grey vennels of windy stone to school, laughter
Flapping about their heads as easily as their hair.
They leave in boatloads; half of them are
    shipwrecked
In Glasgow and London – never come home again.
Today I took a bus by the back roads and watched
    the hills
Thundered by storm, as the light came through the
    rainclouds
In huge moments of gold, pouring across the
    sounds.
And I wondered if perhaps all that was important
    remained after all
Written here in the runes of the water, the land, the
    air,
In a language we no longer know.

⊠ FREEDOM

After night, Edinburgh is spiced with frost.
The morning's blue, so pale it's almost white,
The oval of the moon above
Frail as the face of an old woman.

And in among the pearl-carved pillars and the
    plinths
Of Princes Street, the homeless sleep;
Underneath the doorways and the stairs they curl
Like hedgehogs.

As the wind picks up they shift and dig
A little deeper in their blankets, and some wake up
And blink and stare as I pass by.

As if their voices too have turned to ice,
As if they have forgotten where they are;
They do not even ask for money, only stare
Away into the April air.

And as I go I wonder,
If Scotland's freedom means a jot to them,
On this cold morning as they feel the empty gnaw
Of hunger, and the wind biting at their fingers and
    their faces
Like a dog.

THE STATE OF SCOTLAND

See this land through a broken window,
All huddled in mist, rocked by storm,
The whole long drudge of winter.

Half its people want to leave;
The other half who want to stay
Don't choose, they have no choice.

Our history is written in the hills. We are filled
With pride for what we think we did
And guilt for what we didn't do.

We drift into cities since we cannot stand
The sound of our own thoughts. We spend our lives
Being loud, and trying to forget.

Do we want freedom or just the chance
To mourn not having it? We are willing to fight
For all that we don't want.

◈ PEARLS

They were the reason the Romans came here –
River things, spun into milky globes over years and
     years.
I often wonder who it was who found them first,
Those mussels, dark shells whorled and folded
Like hands in prayer, embedded in feet of shingle.

The travellers knew where they were. The unsettled
     people
Who followed the seasons, the stars, yearned only
     the open road.
They carried the knowledge of pearls inside them,
     secret,
Could tell the very bend of river each pearl had come
     from –
This one like the pale globe of Venus at dawn,
This one a skylark's egg, and this the blush of a
     young girl's lips.

Yet the Romans never reached the Highland rivers
Where the best pearls slept. They were kept out
By the painted people, the Pictish hordes
Bristling on the border like bad weather.

The pearls outlived even the travellers, whose
     freedom
Was bricked into the big towns long enough ago,
Who did not understand any longer
The language of the land.

In the last part of the north,
In the startling blue of the rivers
The shells still grow. Their pearls are stories
That take a hundred years to tell.

◈ Soldier

I see you now, eighteen,
A blond curl of smile, bird's eggs eyes –
No wrong in you except the one motorbike spin
At midnight, when Peter and you came home next
　　morning
Feet awkward and too big, your hands confused.

Now you're going to war;
You stand on the lawn in your uniform
With the cherry trees laughing behind you,
And you don't look a man at all
But a boy in a beautiful play.

What will they do to you there?
What things will you see done on wires
That will haunt you for ever?
What things will you do for your country
You never knew were in your hands?

Breathe this blue wind a last time, boy,
Before you leave, and put this spring day
Deep in the safety of your heart
Like a photograph, to fray and tatter, precious –
For you will not come back this way again.

◈ 1914

It was a Saturday in October
And I had gone out in the sharp pain of bare feet
To the fields all starred with frost,
My mother's bucket thumping at my knee
For water from the well.

Something made me turn to the stables –
Perhaps to whisper my good morning to their
    shadows –
But mostly to crouch in the warm smell of their
    hugeness,
See the black shining of their flanks,
Their heads soft under my hand.

But nothing. Just their scent left
In the grey light scarring from the beams;
The hay yellowing the far wall, untouched,
And old Harry crying softly on an upturned stool
As somewhere a bell mourned six long times.

I did not know where they had gone then
But I cried too, somehow I understood,
Heard on the wire of the wind the sound of guns
And felt our horses, our loved lost horses
Flailing through mud, the terrible waste of mud.

THE WEST HIGHLAND

Every night I asked my mother
To take me to see the train.

Just sometimes
We climbed through the rain's fine tickle,

The black panthers of night,
To look down on our town

Lying in its own shingling of lights,
The ships jewelled and loaded

Furrowing out to sea
In slow hugeness.

At the top of the hill we waited –
My heart beat time –

Till there, necklacing behind the houses,
That golden honeycomb

Trailing north,
Long before I understood what North was,

But felt yet a tug of journeys deep inside,
Pulling through every breath,

As the train melted into mist,
Like something that had never been,

Letting the dark fold back in echoes,
Leaving my feet standing –

In an empty platform,
In a town going nowhere.

◈ Shoes

The shoemaker stitched and sewed
In the dark scent of his own world. Once a year
I went in there, to the black adverts for boots and
    polish
Rusty over the walls of his shop. I blinked

Like something that had tumbled down a hole
Into the heart of the earth. Even the air was tanned,
The chestnut of shoes burnished and perfect from
    hands
That had poured in the pure oils of their love,

Their labour. He wiped those huge hands on his
    apron,
Stood as I smoothed my feet into the mended shoes,
Looking, his eyes like a calf's, brown,
In an air that was brown, a brown cave.

The scent of leather hung in the air
In my shoes that were good as new,
That fitted my feet like hooves –
They shone so I saw my own smile.

I went out into the blue breeze of the springtime,
Watching my step, all the way home. Still,
School scuffed them and skinned them,
Reduced them at last to a shadow of all they had
    been.

18

◈ THE SEA CHANGE

I look back into the house
And see the boy who all that barefoot summer
Came inside for sunset, could not sleep
Because June curtains breathed with light.

A blue breeze that was washed in sea
Brought in pale shells and tided morning;
He walked through wooden rooms and left
Soft footprints under gulls, the skies' wide shores.

And yet inside those days of endless miles
He cried, and did not know why he should cry,
When all the grasses' flowers rubbed his feet
And deep the seas came back to heal his hands.

When now I look at him I think he knew
That childhood broke upon the seas that year
And left sharp spars and masts upon the rocks
And splinters in his eyes.

❖ RUMBLING BRIDGE

One summer afternoon you go
Up the silvering of the river, low
Under the green cathedral of the leaves
Lemoned by sunlight, the slow wheel of gold
High in the huge sky.
Up there, above the flutes of the falls
You lower yourself into the delicious gasp of river
Rock downwards through stone gullies,
Fleeces of water, deep runnels, curls and eddies,
Smoothings the colour of whisky.
You stay water-tobogganing the whole day long until
    the sun
Has bled to death behind the hills,
Till the wind whispers in the trees, shudders them,
And everything is only different shades of blue.
You trail home with sandshoes
As a slip of moon lifts over the pine trees
And the bats weave their own mime through June
    air.
You come home and stand
And don't want to go inside,
Don't want to close your door on this day
Till the last of the light is lost.

KILMELFORD

A bit of country soft with rain
Smelling green, ringing like glass
With the songs of warblers and wrens.

Through thigh-deep wheat fields
Columba's chapels lie still in prayer,
Fallen in on themselves with age.

Now at nightfall the boats sleep
With the white glows of their lamps
Leaning out over August lochs.

The stars flow into the water of the skies
Like pearls from a broken necklace
And the light is long, the night is huge.

 JURA

From Carsaig you can see it,
Three peaks rising up out of the Atlantic,
Like a sea monster, the ridge of a dragon's back.
What is there to find but a scattering of houses,
A road, a hotel, then nothing.
It drifts into mist, a huge loneliness,
Composed of bracken and moor and cave.
Who comes to look? Who bothers
To cross the few sea miles
To watch some great mound of empty stone
Drift into the distance?
This busy world would think it worthless –
A barren landfall on the edge of sanity.
To me it is wondrous that such things should still
    remain,
Uncharted and untamed, like eagles.

◈ SELKIES

He found it out of reach of the sea
In the early morning of May –

A sealskin, salt pod dry,
Smooth as a rush of silk.

His smile twisted and he took it
Home to a chest in the eaves.

That night, at star time,
She shadowed the door, dark-eyed,

A stranger, something in her voice,
Like one shipwrecked from Spain.

All the next day with the horses
He sweated and could not forget –

Came home like a boy, still burning,
To find her beside the hearth.

That midsummer the fiddlers came,
The dancing went all through the night.

A son she bore him, a boy,
A lonely thing, and wild,

Who trailed the stormy beaches,
Dragging a stick and singing –

His son,
Yet never his son at all.

Then one market he took the cart,
Rocked the four shore miles

In a scattering of curlews and lapwings –
The new year rousing like a girl.

When he came home the door was wide
A stillness dark in the windows;

He turned in time to catch
On the blue breath of the sea,

Two seals lifting and falling,
Singing into the deep.

☒ NOVEMBER

Seven years old. All night he's listened
To the great Atlantic wind bullying the house;
He's slept in its paws, been lifted in its ship
Through the long hours to dawn.

At six he gets up and opens a corner of the dark,
Sees a smudge of sky the colour of a dragon's eye
Waking in the far east. He drags on
The rough warmth of a woollen jumper.

He listens for his father's sleep. There's nothing
But the big march of the hall clock.
He whispers down the wooden stairs one by one
Clicks shut the door to the porch.

The cold butts him like an angry ram,
Snatches his breath. He stands for a minute,
Wishing he was back in the snug of his bed,
Deep in dreams.

But it's too late now;
He mutters something he heard the ferryman say
And he feels big, he feels ten years old –
As strong as the storm.

He runs into the wind and it's all about him;
He's a kite, flapping and whirling
Up in the air, up in the dawn skies,
He closes his eyes and laughs.

Bit by bit the light comes;
His uncle's croft lifts out of the gloom
Like a wary wildcat. The ferry comes alive
On its first crossing from Mull.

He's too tired to run the last of the way –
Just walks,
Small, still seven years old
Towards the sound of the sea.

The beach. St Columba's Bay
And a whole white thunder
Rubbling the boulders, the hills of shingle –
There's a sting of salt on his cheek.

He scrabbles down to the water's edge
Keeping one eye on the waves
That come snapping like sheepdogs at his heels,
Tousled paws and heads.

There, a piece of green –
He steals it from under the wave,
And his arm's a torrent of water.
He doesn't so much as notice,

But staggers back and holds the bit of stone
Between forefinger and thumb.
The first pale light of the east
Yellows it, turns the smooth serpentine

To a pure green sun. He gasps, triumphant,
Presses it deep in a pocket
And a wave shudders over his boots
In a deluge of melted Antarctic.

He goes back up the beach
Trying not to cry.
The cold hurts like a cut,
He whimpers till the blood beats back.

Now he sifts though the piles of shingle,
Watching for eyelets of green and yellow
That shine among knuckles of granite and agate,
Polished by years at sea.

Then he turns, squinting,
As a watery flicker of sun
Streams out through the mainland hills
To bathe the beach in morning.

They'll be up. He goes, reluctant,
A half dozen best bits of treasure
Hot in one hand, a hundred others
Heavy in trouser pockets.

They look up from their porridge
When he comes in. His dad sighs,
Moves the paper from his place,
Fixes him with a single eye.

The boy says nothing.
He eats his breakfast, bangs the back door,
Leaves a single oval of emerald
To tell its own story.

❖ SALMON

You are the Atlantic, the personification of currents
    and spates,
You are made of fathoms of water,
Spring runs, Highland rivers –
You have your life's journey ravelled inside you.

I have been to stand on rock ledges
In the fierce rains of autumn;
I have looked down on kettledrums of river
Tumbled to white noise –

And there, up out of this tantrum,
You leap, pouring the source of your being,
The blunt thrust of your head,
Into an impossible return, the river's beginning.

◈ ISLAND

Six hundred miles north, and forty years behind,
London is just a hiss on the radio;
Distant and out of touch.

What matters is the gale battering Camus Lurgan,
The children stranded, the sea too mad to sail,
An old man ill in the village.

Here and there a cottage clings to the hills,
A heather tuft of smoke ruffling its chimney,
The peat stacked to a beehive outside.

At their doors, black and white fleeces of collies,
Tumbled by the wind, their eyes blue as lochs –
Tongues like hot bacon.

The old people have a smattering of English
Like the bits and pieces of crockery
That are kept for the Sabbath.

This place is left at the end of the century –
Intact, brittle – as precious as the lapwing chicks
Fluffed on the spring ground.

✦ GALWAY

and suddenly the light coming in gusts
sweeping out over the sea;
the wild irises with their yellow heads
on silver water, on black water,
the duck rising in stretches, in parallel,
against the limestone shoulders of the hills –
their shale grey strangeness –
before the cloud bruises, the rain scatters
in muslin veils and all is wintered
on this journey, this voyage through moments,
that catch for a second like sunlight
to be beheld and marvelled
before all of it changes and your hands are empty;
only the memory
left as light as the imprint of a leaf
upon your life
for ever.

◈ ORANGES

Sometimes in the summer I would come into the cool, dark well of the kitchen to find my mother. The odd straw sunbeam would find its way through the window and dance like liquid gold on the floor.

On one surface the fruit bowl stood, full of pears and oranges. I loved the scent of the oranges most of all; I put them right to my nose and sniffed, and into my head there came vivid colours: blues and yellows and brilliant white.

I asked my mother where the oranges came from. *Africa*, she said. I had no idea where Africa was, but the sound of the word reverberated through my head in the cool of the kitchen, and behind my eyes pictures came of a place full of magical birds and stories and people, people with oranges in their hands.

◈ THE STAR

There was once a man called Kay who discovered a
star. He found it in his telescope and it was golden,
the colour of a Sri Lankan topaz. He watched it and
watched it for he knew that this was his star, that this
was the first time astronomers and scientists had
ever known of its existence. And the star was called
after him – Kay's Star.

The man grew older. For a time magazines
remembered the anniversary of his discovery, and
it was as if his star came back into orbit. But then,
one by one, they began to forget. New things were
discovered: better ways of playing music, quicker
ways of cooking food, easier ways of making money.
Kay's Star grew less bright; it flickered on the edge of
the sky and began to grow faint and grey.

The man could not care for himself any more. He
was put into an old people's home where nurses
said, "Could you lift your hands, Mr Kay?" and, "Now
we'll soon have you into your bath, won't we?" Every
night in the ward he looked out of the window, for
his bed was nearest it, at the stars that crusted the
huge heavens. And his eyes wandered across the
blue-black, searching always for the star which he
had found and which now was lost.

◈ THE PALACE

The river ran out of the mountain in a flute, a white
plume. That winter, the one that will never be
forgotten, the river froze. Nobody saw the second
the river broke into ice, nobody was there. But the
following day it had become already a cave of ice, a
cave that was becoming many caves and chambers
as the water kept on plinthing from the opening of
the river and freezing as it began to fall. At night the
ice caves were lit against the huge golden burning
of the skies; they became like amber honeycombs
through which trespassers might walk and watch.
Every day there were new galleries, new roofs, new
windows. But there was no-one there.

◈ THE DREAM

That night the moon was silver, but weird and eerie
– it raced through the clouds above the ship like
the mad eye of a dead god. All through the watch
there was nothing except the lift and creak of the
stern, and strange glimmerings on the water like
little lightnings where the moon fell. When I went
back down into the hold at dawn the men slept as
if entranced; their heads rolled sideways and their
eyes tight fastened. And next morning they spoke
of the same dream, of dreaming the same dream,
the dream I have spent the last forty years of my life
trying to comprehend, of a field blowing with wheat
and the shadow of a man who does not show his
face.

 SUMMER

Summer is about seeing a girl of four out of the corner of a side window going contentedly about the spading of sand into a bucket as her father murmurs beside her and the sun falls on the slats of the house in a lemon-orange Saturday way in the middle of Michigan.

WALDORF

It is mid-October and in southern Germany they
are gathering apples. They are still on the hillside at
eight o'clock in the evening and the tractor that is
more than thirty years old has lamps on its bumpers
and roof so the three men who are working can see.
The air is filled with the scent of bruised apples and
fallen leaves. It is a scene Monet would have painted,
but Monet would not have been able to capture the
soft laughter of the men as they bend for another
load of fruit, nor the muffled echoes of the church
bells as they ring out eight times across the long
valley.

 # EDGE

If you drive to the west coast there is one special
road you must take. It is a single track road and
there are many potholes in it, for it would seem that
no-one else has driven that way for a long, long time.

Drive there in May, when the sky at the edge of the
horizon is blue, a very light and washed-out blue
that I know is the colour of a certain bird's egg. Drive
slowly and open all the windows, and you will hear
the larks stringing their songs like magnificent harps
in the air, and you will hear the wind passing over
the meadows like a woman's hand.

The rocks are all white and made of limestone, and
out of them grow flowers bright as drops of blood.
Here and there in secret dells there are whole
villages of orchids, their trumpets white and mauve
and gold.

Then at last you will come to a place beyond which it
is impossible to drive. Leave the car and wander over
the meadow that lies to the left until you see the sea.
Then run until you reach it.

❖ SEEING

It was on the third night he realised. He woke up on the bare hillside and the moonlight was silvering everything around him. Here and there things were shimmering close by. He got out of his sleeping bag and began going from one piece of shining to the next. They were pieces of metal, twisted and melted. He realised in the end that he was in the very middle of a plane crash. All night he lay awake, staring up at the sky, trying to put the pieces back together.

⌧ LAURENCEKIRK

The lapwings are back in the low sky
Across the crumbled fields of spring
As a torn sun glitters the new-ploughed earth
And snowflake gulls flurry behind the tractor's
    lurch.
Scotland is coming bleary from her sleep;
Like a mother that's given birth, weary,
Her eyes are slowly coming round, unclouding,
As rain scorns a hill there, and braids of rainbow
Celebrate the greyness of the far North Sea.
But always, always, the lapwings tumble in the bright
    new fields
And now, as always, I don't know
Whether they laugh or weep.

THE LILY

Last year we dug the pond –
Heaved up roots, old wire and pots,
Smoothed the deep ground, lined it,
Let water flow into its hold like liquid glass.
Your family gave you the lily for Christmas;
All winter it slept in the water,
Through the fierce blue days of January,
When ice grew thick as a doorstep there
And it seemed it would be winter for eternity.
But the year flowed slowly back in time,
Melted into the first blossom of spring,
And the geese struggled the skies for Iceland.
We had forgotten all about the lily until,
One day, it opened its heart in the middle of the sun
Like a princess, and we marvelled, laughed, came
        close
In wonderment as if some baby star
Had crashed into our grass and stayed alight.
For four whole days we were like our own children
And the lily was the centre of the world.

⊠ CLARSACH

They had scarcely noticed her before.
A slip of a thing no more than sixteen,
A glitter of eyes and auburn hair –
It was November and they wanted nothing
But the peat fire and a whiskied head.
That first night she played the heads turned,
Fell away from their loose talk;
One by one they heard a rippling
Like the shudder of breeze over the black loch,
Like the unfurling of swans.
It was her hands –
The grace and flow of the fingers
Playing with the taut stems of the strings.
They saw their own hands then,
Lumped and ruddy, knuckled with fights.
She played them quiet. Like a long wave
She washed them ashore to the island
Where she wanted them, beached them
Dry and wondering, dog-eyed,
In the long echo that was left behind.

 ARGYLL

All down the coast
The air was full of fish and sunset.

By nine the lemon-coloured cottages
Were warm windows glowing over the bays.

Far west the light a rim of blue and white,
Jura and Mull and Scarba all carved from shining.

On the way home we stopped to listen to the dark,
To the sea coming huge over a hundred beaches.

In among the trees, in windless stillness,
The bats were flitting, weaving patterns with the air.

That night I did not want the stars to rise at all
I wanted it to be like this and nothing more

Looking west into the sunset
To the very end of the world.

▧ J ULY

In July go up to the attic
And fetch down the canvas bag
Next to the one with the Christmas lights;
Bring it down and smell in the fabric
Old lochs, old reeds.
Try the reel, dry it from waxy sleep.
Listen for the fingertips of rain on the corrugated
      iron of the shed
And put your head round the closed warmth of the
      door
To say you'll be back late. Take the flask,
Jumpers, your best coat and boots,
And simply start into the hills behind the house.
There's not a breath of wind;
An eagle floats in a gold brooch
Somewhere above Scarp,
And for a second, a ledge of sunlight, rusted,
Swivels the hills behind Rodel.
After five hundred feet of toiling
The breeze is bliss on your brow,
The midges are dancing a jig,
Mocking as you stand breathless
And all of a sudden it's there –
Dark blue in the clasp of the moorland,
Grazed by an edge of breeze, its rowans
Wind-shaped, leaning away from the west.
You come home in the first mauve shadows,
Your hands still smelling of that one fish
Made of water, of reeds, of stones –
Slippery, as hard to catch as the story.

⬧ THE TENNIS COURT

That summer the blue heat never moved
But lay heavy as iron on the island.
Odd days we dragged over tracks
To combs of sea crashing long across the beaches
And waded out, burned by a blissful sting of cold.
In the evenings, curlews trailed their songs of pearls
Over the whole horizon; in all the open windows
The blue breeze murmured like a shell against the
        ear.

Then that day I rounded a corner in the wood
And found the tennis court. Lying out of time,
Half shrubbed by a sway of grass, the net
Like a muslin thing from days of empire,
The lines alive and still remembering –
Ladies and gentlemen whose white laughter
Lay buried somewhere underneath
Another summer and another world.

❖ Two Years Old

Under the chestnuts of summer
Beside the waters of a lake
They decide it's the end of the road
That each has had enough.

The house in London will be halved
Candlesticks broken up
The books split down the middle
Their sideboard sawn in two.

She will tear out
Seventy percent of his heart
Fathor will get the rest –
This is a division of love.

But Louis will bleed and bleed
From the wound they leave behind –
Until he understands
This is how grown-ups are.

◈ A Story

The light at the edge of the sky,
The last swallows skirting the air;
We walk down and down and down
Until we walk into a painting.

All of our lives we have been getting there,
To that one field at nightfall;
Four different roads
To meet that June.

To stand in the hayfield – new-cut and smelling of
      blondeness –
The stubble beneath our feet sore;
To stretch up into the cherry trees and pick
Shining red moons of cherries.

It feels like being a child again;
Inside a bale of hay I scent
The memory of a girl I knew when I was six,
A summer so far away.

And I know that one day this too will be a story,
A painting in my head, a place both real and not,
Lying, beautiful, in the books of my eyes,
To be returned to, as long as there is light.

❖ MOON

We came back at midnight from Bangor
The moon playing tig with us

Pouring solid silver over the Menai Straits
Then powering though clouds

Blinking behind trees until we were home
Thudded the car doors shut

Looked up through the warm October darkness
Over the aimless wandering of hedges

To a whole moon softened by clouds
Flying like a kite at the end of a string

Over Anglesey, turning the whole huge sky
Into something burnished, scorching the stars

Leaving the fields underneath steel-white
Bright, magic, light enough to walk

All the way to the sea
All the way to morning.

ORTA

For always the word will fill my mouth
With soft water, harbours,
The skulled eyes of windows,
Staring from buildings that lean from an island

In late evening. Saying farewell will be
The swift white furl of a boat –
Yellows and oranges melting
From the piers and the upstairs rooms.

I have seen the firing of white eyes
In the young day of their loves
Like candles at the tables of Orta;
I have felt the huge drag of anchors inside me

That pain at the weight of being –
Longing to break, to rise,
To stop being afraid and sing
With the whole blood of freedom.

A boat lies at the end of a street
Cupped by the water. It is ten o'clock;
I am going home, but I am not sure
I know where that is any more.

❖ SEPTEMBER

The fields lay white beneath a snow of sun
And birds were restless underneath, they rose and
    wheeled
Like silver leaves. The skies were more than blue;
Burnished and beaten with a strange brilliance.
The angels are coming, I thought;
The angels will come in the night
When a huge moon ovals through these bright and
    cloudless skies;
They will come to bind the sheaves
While we are fast asleep.
They will work the fields, their wings tight-folded,
All through the white night of this September,
The moon gliding high like a balloon
Over the glazed harvest of the world;
Nothing moving except the angels and the wind,
    until the task is done
In the warm stillness of the dawn.

◈ ST KILDA

Always in winter the fiddle tunes came
When the wind shone bright on the headlands,
Grazing the eye, battling about the house at night,
Mad and almighty.

He lay there in the small hours before dawn,
And the Atlantic swelled through the room,
Bringing in its fingers stories of far away,
Of long ago, of make believe.

And the notes swam into his hands,
They chased and danced, little chinks of things,
Till he heard them, till they crammed his head
With a whole symphony of song.

He took his fiddle and fought for them,
Listened, his ear catching the Atlantic,
Searching and sifting the right note
Before it faded away for ever.

By the time morning had blown back from the sea,
Lay grey and dazed in the window,
The tune was done, was drying,
Like a fish net in the wind.

⊞ THE HORSEMAN'S WORD

He did not know French or the history of art.
He did not know the declensions of verbs.
He did not know when Sir Christopher Wren
Built the dome of St Paul's Cathedral.

He knew the names of the songbirds,
He knew where the geese came to rest in autumn,
And he knew the one word
That could bridle a wild horse;
The word that had passed like a pearl
From mouth to mouth, son after son,
That secret whisper old as the fields themselves.

When his father lay
Washed up on the last tide of his life,
He gave his word
To the young, bright, blue well of a boy,
Who caught it and kept it,
Let it flow into the strong blood of his growing.

And later, when a whole galloping of horses
Had softened under his voice,
They envied him black
On the farms where they had books and learning
    and stables;
They stared at him dumb, bewildered,
As he broke their stallions from wild thrashings of
    river
To beautiful waterfalls, creatures that poured

Into one word's gallop, that stilled
At the weight of a single hand.

He kept his word, his pearl,
Deep in the dark of his head –
A whole inheritance.

▣ THE ARTISTS

Her father sold canvases in Paris
In the black and white days before war
Drowned the young men of Europe
In the mud of their own blood.
He sold canvases to the artists
Who lived down dark nowheres
In bare attics and huddled cellars.
He watched them go from the shop, shaking his head
At the yellow stains of their fingers
The old smell of their clothes.
He knew the hard bargain of money
They failed to comprehend.

But one night in July
He saw them leave for the country
His canvases in their bags,
And the gourd of the moon poured over them,
Poured over them and their laughter.
He stood there, alone and dark,
As they went searching the sound of the wheat,
The colour of the air,
The scent of the starlight.

◈ After All

He sits, waiting for his own death,
In the stubborn chair that has been his
For forty years. Ask him what happened
In June of 1932 and he will tell you
With words sharp as bullets, hard as lead –
His grey eyes will fierce you with their power.
It's the older years that just desert him now –
All his yesterdays rise up like geese across the Solway
Dissolve against the Irish Sea.
The doctor cannot heal himself (has forgotten how),
When names and dates and faces flow away
And someone else's writing reminds him who will
        call,
Who will bring his meal, what time to go to bed.
Once upon a time he strode the long, blue beaches
That now lie useless in his windows;
All he can hear are curlews
Calling his name as the dark uncurls its blanket
And the stars come out like grains of salt
In the sore wounds of the sunset.

◈ THE WOUND IN THE EARTH

All day under the circling
The golden hugeness of the sun
Beat by beat the maddening, terrible day
The terrible madness, until, suddenly, at last
The sky went ugly with bruises, a thunder stuttered
In the red hills and the rain came hard as grapes
Heavy, hissing, huge, and lightning gouged the dust.
His face, she saw his face, her son
The son she'd brought into a stable
Shining with bright rain and blood in rivers
And how his head slipped forwards, finished
His shoulders torn like wings, like angel wings
Broken now for ever by the weight
Of this last loss of God.
But even then they waited, the soldiers and the
    priests
Watching him with gaping mouths as if they still
    expected
He might speak or heal or teach.
They watched the rain shine his shoulders and his
    broken head
Hour after hour after hour
As if they feared him still.

◈ Her Morning

It has rained for days –
Choirs have sung from roofs and windows,
The lanes are knee-deep in November.
But this morning, this Sunday morning,
The rain glitters in mica
When sunlight opens like a bud across the fields.

Once upon a time it snowed in mid-November –
Great soft kittens' paws of snow that spun
Out of a grey-dark sky until
The house crouched more than silent,
Like some gigantic snowball in the woods.
He came and asked if she would go for holly.

Half-dark the woods, the stars like seeds,
Pale in a frightened sky. She holds his hand –
He smells of pipesmoke, moss, old books and cloth –
And suddenly he is her father
And she is six years old
Her sledge thudding at her back, her feet too small.

The holly cuts their hands with shiny spines,
Those berries the same colour as the beads
That bleed their fingers. At last
Her hands are wounds, all red and raw,
Yet never in her life before
Has she felt so alive.

All that was a flock of winters back –
The years have flown like swallows, lifted one on one
And stretched into the darkness of the past.
Only his photograph is left, frozen black and white,
A smile that might be crying –
A broken ledge of time.

Now the whole house echoes
With her aloneness. He never said goodbye;
How does one ever grieve enough for one who's
    gone?
The rain is washing him away,
And in the end the river finds the sea, the journey's
    done –
And all the world is salt.

She goes downstairs and hears the rain has stopped.
The church bells bloom across the fields
And suddenly a gust of sun blows through the trees;
She cannot see, she's blinded by the light –
For a moment she can feel his arms about her,
The dance that whirled her heart.

She breathes his name and he is gone,
And yet she feels his smile
So close it stills her cheek.
She starts towards his absence
Like broken glass – shattered fragments
Refracted by the light.

◈ EASTER IONA

Listen. There is nothing except the wind.
The sheep lie in boulders in the fields,
The first few lambs shelter to the south-east of their
    mothers.
The moon swims through cloud, a rim of gold,
Yet never flows clear into open sky, never burns the
    sea with light.

Is there a God in all this blackness,
The huge emptiness of night? How small we are
When our lights go out, when all we can comfort our
    dark with
Are candles. In the end, each and every invention is
    not sufficient
To cure our loneliness, to take away our fear,
To solve the riddle of death. We can fly to the moon,
But we cannot heal the flaw in a broken soul.

Easter. How we took the only one who ever truly
    knew us
And murdered him. That night the dark must have
    seemed so close,
The emptiness so huge. The disciples
Blown away into huddled corners of Jerusalem,
Their hope broken, their lives lost.

Far away east, a black blood stains the sky;
The cold is bad, like a wound, it hurts the heart,
Twists like a rusted knife. Morning is many miles
    away;
Resurrection, awakening, they seem nothing more
    than a story
In some half-forgotten book, and yet Easter is
    becoming real
A little every second, the candles are being born
    across the hills
Until, at last, they conquer night, they light an
    impossible morning,
A beautiful hope.

◈ DAFFODILS

They flurry over the first raw green of the hills,
Trumpet the Easter fields;
Bright flags with their orange yolks
Bending under the flaying cruelty of April winds.

As if to prove that Calvin got it wrong,
That dark-lipped Luther in the cold austerity of
    history
Threw away the warm laughter of love
For the bare bones of theology.

UNST

Under these huge skies
On the last day of August
We drive between nowhere and nowhere.

Nothing lives in this landscape
Except the stories of those who died here
Written in ruins.

This is north of sanity;
Did everything that matter
Blow away a long time ago?

Yet we go into churches
Built of little but faith,
So thin and flimsy.

A dog, fleeced by the wind,
Tumbles towards his master, is gathered,
As they splinter into rain.

A black facet of loch,
Held in the claws of the loch,
Lit vivid with lilies.

And over there, on the edge of the world,
The sun pours out shining
So bright it cuts the eyes.

◈ Angus Macphee of South Uist

He came from the island
Where there is bread and salt
And a huge sky blowing.
His learning was woven from those things
To wisdom, his own books.

But in the war they sent him to
Something unwound, he lost touch
With what mattered and made sense
To the schoolteacher and the priest
And the men who ploughed the seasons.

He unwound and his big blue eyes
Laughed at the spring light; they saw no longer
All that needed fetching and carrying,
That must build the drystone wall
Of their life against the wind.

So they sent him to the mainland –
The dry land –
A place of white walls and no doors,
Where he was told when he could wash his hands
Or eat his bread or sleep.

And in the dry land were other people
Who rocked backwards and forwards,
Who never stopped talking about nothing,
Whose hands had to be held
For their fear of what was not there.

And his words dried inside him
Like the flowers that blow free
On the island that brought him up.
The words stopped like water in winter
And they all poured into his hands.

In the garden he picked grasses;
He searched for tall grasses with stems,
To weave into the things he was feeling.
He made garments from grass soft as felt
Out of the pictures that grew in his hands.

But no-one could understand his language,
No-one could read his writing,
No-one tried to translate
The wild song he still wove
From the island alive inside him.

Be thou a smooth way before me,
Be thou a guiding star above me,
Be thou a keen eye behind me,
This day, for ever.

St Columba

OTHER TITLES BY KENNETH STEVEN
AVAILABLE FROM SAINT ANDREW PRESS

Iona
(ISBN 0 7152 0778 4)

Wild Horses
illustrated by John Busby
(ISBN 0 7152 0798 9)

Splinters: poems for the Carpenter
illustrated by Sheila Cant
(ISBN 0 7152 0756 3)